Miscarriage Mom

The Unspoken Realities of Miscarriage and How to Cope

Kristy Parisi

authorHOUSE®

AuthorHouse™
1663 Liberty Drive
Bloomington, IN 47403
www.authorhouse.com
Phone: 1 (800) 839-8640

Published by AuthorHouse   12/30/2015

ISBN: 978-1-5049-7126-3 (sc)
ISBN: 978-1-5049-7125-6 (hc)
ISBN: 978-1-5049-7124-9 (e)

Print information available on the last page.

This book is printed on acid-free paper.

To everyone who has lost a baby through miscarriage: may this book bring you comfort and hope in your time of need.

Contents

Acknowledgments

To my husband, Vinny: Words can't express my gratitude for your continuous support and unconditional love. Thank you for always being my rock, my shoulder to cry on, and my reminder that all is not lost. Your ability to look on the bright side in our darkest moments is truly inspirational.

Mum and Dad, thank you for all your love and support. Your e-mails and calls meant more to me than I ever expressed.

Anita, thank you for listening and for never judging my erratic thinking during times of grief. I am blessed to have had you as a friend for the past twenty-three years. I miss you every day.

To Rebecca, my deepest sympathy for the loss of your angel babies. They are never forgotten. Thank you for understanding me when no one else did.

Thank you, Mr. and Mrs. Parisi, for all your love and support over the years. I could not have been blessed with more loving in-laws.

Introduction

My Story

This book is in your hands for a very good reason. Whether you've recently lost a child or someone special to you has lost a child, my hope is that the words and ideas contained here help you find comfort in your loss. Before I can give you advice on how and what you should or could be doing, it's essential that you know a little something about me so that you know my words are genuine and are coming from someone who has experienced the same kind of heartache.

I have just recently celebrated ten years of marriage and my thirty-fourth birthday. My husband and I are what would seem from the outside a fit and healthy young couple. We met while we were both at the peak of our athletic careers. I was a professional softball player; Vinny was a professional baseball player. We were both living in Italy, playing ball, at the time we met.

I had always considered myself healthy and athletic. By no means would I have predicted that I, of all women, would have trouble conceiving and carrying a child to full term. I ate well, I worked out daily, and I was happy and in love. In reality, I was just a normal Aussie chick with short blonde hair, blue eyes, and an accent that causes confusion because it reflects both my Australian heritage and my American life.

I never thought in a million years I would be writing a book on this topic. We all like to think that it's never going to happen to us. And then it does. I lost six babies over a five-year-period through miscarriage.

We started trying to have children when I was twenty-seven. Just three months after going off the contraceptive pill, I fell pregnant. We were ecstatic. I had a positive pregnancy test one early morning, and that afternoon I made an appointment with my doctor. When she confirmed I was pregnant, I broke down in tears of joy.

I met my husband at our local Target, where we picked out a cute onesie that read, "Grandma loves me." I'm always thinking of creative gifts, so this was no exception. This was going to be the first grandchild for both our parents, so we knew how excited they were going to be. Later that evening, we went over to Vinny's parents, and I handed my mother-in-law the gift. She looked confused for a second but soon realized what we were telling her. She too broke down in tears of joy.

Fast-forward one week. I was at the gym, getting ready for a light workout, when I discovered I was bleeding. I panicked and within an hour was back at the doctor's office. She confirmed I had lost the baby.

We were devastated. How? Why? What did I do wrong? I was lost; I couldn't understand how this had happened to me. Nothing anyone said could take away the pain I was feeling. "It's so common these days" seemed to be the go-to piece of advice others gave me.

A short while later, after being cleared by the doctor, we started to try again. Again it didn't take long before I was pregnant. This time it was different. There was no celebration, limited excitement, and a lot of stress. Weeks passed, and things seemed to be going well. We made it past five weeks, which was better than the last time.

Since I had previously experienced a miscarriage, I was privileged to an early ultrasound. At eight weeks, I went in for my first one. I was excited to see my baby on the screen and experience that moment like the moms I saw on TV. It would be perfect.

Or so I thought. The doctor couldn't find a heartbeat or even a sign of my child. She said their machines were a little old and suggested I go to another office, where they had state-of-the-art technology.

The twenty-minute car ride to that office felt like an hour. I think I knew deep down the baby was gone, but I didn't want to believe it and was not ready to accept it. Within an hour of arriving at the office, it was confirmed that the baby had stopped growing. I was heartbroken. Again, no rhyme or reason. It just happens, we were told.

The second miscarriage was even harder to cope with. I was devastated and angry that I had failed again, but I wasn't ready to give up. We continued to try for another baby; but this time we had no luck. A year went by, and I didn't fall pregnant. Every month was filled with both hope and disappointment.

After that year, I decided it was time to see a specialist. A friend recommended her fertility specialist, under whose care she'd undergone IVF and conceived a girl. Within one month of meeting with the specialist, I was pregnant. He actually had nothing to do with it, as we had merely had a consultation— and I was already pregnant for the third time.

Now that I was a patient at a specialist clinic, I was privileged to weekly blood drawings so we could closely watch my HCG (human chorionic gonadotropin) levels. The HCG hormone is made by cells formed in the placenta. It is not normally found in the body, thus the detection of HCG in a home pregnancy test indicates placental cells are present. Without going into detail here, I lost the baby at eight weeks again. This time I had to undergo a dilatation and curettage (D&C). In a D&C, dilatation refers to opening the cervix; curettage refers to removing the contents of the uterus. The surgery itself only takes about 15– 20 minutes. Following surgery you can expect mild menstrual cramps and light bleeding for a week or two. Again, no rhyme or reason—it just happens, we were told.

With each miscarriage, I was more and more devastated. I became very angry. And depression set in. This cycle continued for another two years. We would fall pregnant, I would undergo weekly blood readings, and at around eight weeks, I would lose the baby. This happened three more times for a total of six miscarriages.

I was depressed, exhausted, and defeated. Now thirty-two years old and heavier than I had ever been in my life, I was ready to give up. So I did. I decided I needed to allow myself time to heal. The only way I could let go was to go back on the pill. It was the only way to stop the emotional and mental games every month, every menstrual cycle.

So I went back on the pill and began writing this book. I don't want any woman to ever have to go through pain like I did for so long, so I feel that writing this book is my calling. I'm writing these words to help you.

This is my only wish: that the words contained within this book allow you to grieve, accept, remember, and find comfort in your loss. You aren't alone.

Chapter 1

What to Expect Emotionally

I swear I will punch that pregnant lady in the face if she doesn't stop complaining!

Yes, you read that correctly. Don't be alarmed if you find yourself thinking some awful, crazy thoughts after a miscarriage. For a time, you may experience a change in how you view life. Small things will seem smaller and even insignificant. All you can think about is your child and who he or she could have been. You probably started to consider names for your child, how you were going to decorate the nursery, who would be the godparents, and the like. Miscarriages often occur

1

abruptly; you aren't forewarned that your baby plans won't come to fruition.

Due to the anger and negative emotions building up inside, it's common to experience some outrageous thoughts and feelings that shock you. You may find yourself having an internal conversation, wondering where these thoughts came from. You may even ask yourself, *Who am I?*

Did you walk out of the doctor's office hating every pregnant woman sitting in the waiting area?

I sure did!

Right now, you're most likely feeling pretty angry. Or should I say *very* angry? Angry that you lost your angel. Angry that people don't seem to care. Angry that no one understands you. Angry that the mother in the supermarket is treating her child that way; if only she knew how fortunate she was. Angry that the woman over there is complaining about how hard it is to be pregnant in the summer. You're probably so angry you might actually punch someone if he or she isn't careful. (I don't recommend this, although I totally get it. Try going to the gym instead.)

I'm typically a laid-back person; the small things in life rarely bother me. I do my best to put things in perspective and look at the bigger picture. I tend to handle adversity very well and often have no problem finding something positive in any situation. But that was never the case after a miscarriage.

In the weeks and months after a miscarriage, it was hard for me to let go of the tornado of negative emotions that were building up inside me. *I lost six babies. What's positive about that?* I was very angry, and I was jealous of every mother on this earth. I was jealous of every pregnant woman who got to experience pregnancy and watch her belly grow. I was jealous she got to shop for maternity clothes and baby items. I was jealous of all the young moms playing with their kids in the park.

It's understandable to have these feelings. You've just lost your child due to no fault of your own, and he or she can't be bought back. Please know that these feelings are valid and normal. With time, they will subside, and you will begin to feel like yourself again. I promise. For some, it takes longer than others, and that's okay. In the meantime, if you're having a hard time even looking at a baby, I suggest avoiding places that you know will be swarmed with pregnant women or young children, if possible.

For me, along with anger and jealously came an overwhelming feeling of sadness. You're mourning, and it's okay to be sad. It's important to find someone you can talk to, who understands your loss and will listen to you. Don't bottle up your feelings of sadness. It's okay to cry.

Surround yourself with a support system to help you move forward. I wanted to be alone, and that's okay. However, you can't be alone forever; it's against our human nature. Talking about it is also important. I didn't talk to anyone about my loss. I tried to keep myself together and put on a strong face. This led me down the path to depression. I don't want you to go there. Trust me, it's neither fun nor healthy. Allow yourself to feel these feelings, and then do your best to let them go, and move forward. With time, you'll begin to feel your normal self again.

Then something happens.

Just as you're starting to feel like you're doing better, someone says something or does something that takes you right back to where you started.

Angry and upset.

During my second pregnancy, my sister-in-law was also pregnant. In fact, our due dates were only two weeks apart. I lost my baby at eight weeks. Months passed, and I was doing okay. Then my mother-in-law asked me to write the invitations for my sister-in-law's baby shower. I adore my mother-in-law, so without hesitation, I said yes. But when I sat down to write the invitations, it hit me. I was a mess.

The horrible, negative feelings crept right back into my life. *How could they ask me to write these invitations? I should be writing my own baby shower invitations. Has everyone already forgotten I too was pregnant? My baby should be due too.* I sat there and cried as I handwrote each invitation. I suggest that if someone asks this of you, kindly remind her you don't think it's the best idea and gently refuse the offer.

I wrote the invitations, and I attended the baby shower. The baby shower was for my niece, after all. But with every game played and every gift opened, I felt anger building back up inside. Was I being selfish? Shouldn't I have been happy? Was I a bad person for not wanting to be there? Looking back, I know it was not wrong of me to have those feelings.

If you're in a similar situation—maybe your sister or best friend is also pregnant, and you find yourself in this internal debate—try to hold yourself together. Do whatever you need to do. If you need to walk away, walk away. If you need to decline an invitation, kindly decline. I didn't want to be rude or cause a scene, as it was my sister-in-law's special day, so I sat through all the festivities of the day.

Looking back now, I know I could have left. They would have understood that it was too soon for me to be writing baby shower invitations and watching baby gifts being opened. Speak up for what you know you can and can't take. You don't have to be a hero and put on an act. Family and friends will understand if you let them know what's going on inside. Don't put yourself through any more than you have already been through.

As time passes and you begin to accept your loss (not forget it) and move on, you will no longer feel like punching that pregnant woman in the face. Gradually you can be surrounded once again by things baby without breaking down into a ball of sadness.

The Dreaded Question

You get married, and you know it's coming. It may come from your parents, friends, or veritable stranger. For some reason, people feel inclined to ask couples without children, "So, when are you guys going to have kids."

Ouch!

I've experienced this many times over. My family and close friends know we've tried to have a child and understand our situation, so we don't get it a lot. When Vinny and I meet new people and they find out we are in our midthirties and just celebrated our tenth wedding anniversary, for some reason the next questions are child related: *Do you guys have kids? No. So, when are you guys going to have kids?*

Although this questioning is seemingly unavoidable, it hurts. It's rude for *anyone* to ask questions of this manner, because none of us know the histories of everyone we meet. Our accomplishments and failures aren't written on our faces. Behind every person is a story, and people need to respect that.

I try to focus only on the things I can control, and I can't control whether a stranger is going to ask such a question. However, I can choose how I react. I prefer to tell the truth. Though this may seem awkward to you, your miscarriage is not something you should hide—unless you choose to keep it private. In that case, you may like to say something as simple as "I don't know" and then change the subject.

You shouldn't feel ashamed or feel like you can't answer truthfully because of how the topic of miscarriage makes others feel. It's a part of life for millions of couples and shouldn't be taboo. When I mention this to other women, I often find they too have miscarried. Immediately a special bond is formed. It's nice to know others out there have been down the same road. I believe women should help and support each other, and one way to do this is by not hiding our struggles.

What exactly do I say? I tell them straight up: "Oh, we tried, but I've had six miscarriages." If the person you're speaking with hasn't experienced a miscarriage, then he or she is likely to cringe and apologize, but it is what it is.

While we're discussing stray comments that are too frequently thrown out there without any thought behind them, let's look at that one thrown out most often by tired parents. On more than one occasion, I've been standing in line at the grocery store alongside young kids misbehaving, begging their parent for every and any candy bar conveniently placed by the cash register. Often embarrassed, the parent will nonchalantly say to me, "You want them? You can take them."

Ouch! Dagger to the heart.

Don't cry! Don't cry!

Depending on the time frame between these comments and your miscarriage, it can be very upsetting. Please know that if you find yourself in one of these situations, feeling hurt or angry is understandable. You aren't being irrational for having these feelings. People don't realize their comments are potentially heartbreaking to a woman who has recently miscarried. In this situation, I leave everything unsaid. There's no need to add fuel to the exhausted parent's fire.

Chapter 2

Facing the World Again

Did you ever walk into a room and all conversation stopped? Did the room fill with an awkward silence? Don't worry; you aren't alone. This often happened after one of my miscarriages. People didn't seem to know how to react when they heard the news. When someone passes, people know to send sympathy cards and give caring words to the grieving family. However, when a woman miscarries, people tend to freeze, not knowing what to do or what to say. No one came rushing to my door with words of sympathy. I believe, for the most part, people just don't know what to say. So they take the safe route and say nothing at all.

It's interesting to look back on how people reacted. Most reactions were unexpected or at least different from what I'd consider appropriate. And these reactions occurred again and again. I wondered if it was me, if I was doing something to cause people to react in certain ways. But when my best friend miscarried her first child, she got the same reactions. I live in Florida, and she lives in Perth, Western Australia, so I realized the issue is worldwide. I was comforted that it wasn't just me.

Generally, society seems confused about how to react to the loss of a child through miscarriage. This chapter helps prepare you for some of the not-so-comforting reactions, so you can deal with them if they occur. I've broken them into particular groups, as people's reactions vary depending on their closeness to you.

Our families are typically the people we feel we can rely on the most. They're the ones we expect to know exactly what to do and say to help ease our pain. Hopefully, that has been the case for you. Unfortunately, though miscarriages are common, the event is foreign to anyone who hasn't experienced it. Sometimes family members are no more qualified to comfort you than anyone else.

Partners and Spouses

If you're blessed with a spouse or loving partner, you'll most likely share your pain with him first. For many years, I cried to my husband about how life is unfair and asked what I did wrong. "Why does this keep happening to us?"

Naturally, as a male, he tried to fix the problem. He'd ask, "What can I do to make you happy? Do you want me to go get you something?" He didn't like to see me cry and needed to know how to make it stop. He needed to know how to fix my unhappiness in that moment. What I needed from him was a listening ear and understanding—not for him to fix it. There was nothing to fix; no one can fix grieving. It wasn't until my last miscarriage (baby number six) that my husband did exactly what I needed.

Because of my history (five miscarriages in five years), doctors intervened with my desire to have a child, and we were together doing everything possible to ensure the next pregnancy went full term. I was seven weeks pregnant, and my HCG numbers weren't increasing as much as expected in a healthy pregnancy. I underwent weekly blood tests to monitor these levels. Each visit to the doctor's office was as nerve-racking as giving a speech to a thousand people. I always had to take a deep breath right before answering the doctor's call with that week's numbers. I was stressed, desperate, and on edge.

One Friday, a nurse called to say my numbers were not up from the week before, indicating I would likely lose the baby. The fact my HCG levels had not gone down was the only glimmer of hope that the baby might make it. But everything pointed toward an ectopic pregnancy. An ectopic pregnancy is a pregnancy in which a fertilized egg develops outside the uterus, typically in the fallopian tube. This is known to happen in about one of every fifty pregnancies. Doctors usually discover it by the eighth week of pregnancy. The nurse continued to warn me of all the side effects I needed to watch for over the weekend—things like pain under the breast; heavy, unusual bleeding; and severe pain in the abdomen, shoulder, and so on. I was on high alert and was told to go directly to the emergency room if I felt any of the above. Happy Friday!

Vinny is from a loud and loving Italian family. Every Sunday night, the entire family eats a big Italian meal together at his parents' house. His dad makes the best meatballs—the size of your fist. After dinner, I shared our baby's grim situation. I was happy to have made it through the weekend with no symptoms. Monday morning, I headed back to the doctor's office with high hopes. I'd be lying, however, if I said I wasn't scared about what was to come.

At the doctor's office, I was told it was, in fact, an ectopic pregnancy. The baby was gone. I was devastated. The nurse informed me that, to treat the ectopic pregnancy, she would give me two shots to help "everything" pass. She explained, "It's quite a large shot, so we will be doing one on each side." I was to put all my weight on the opposite side of my body when it was time.

I was wearing a heavy hoodie and asked the nurse if I should remove it to make it easier for her to access my upper arm.

"Oh no," she said, "it goes in the gluteus. Can you please pull down your pants?"

I didn't see that one coming.

Leaving the doctor's office with a Band-Aid on each butt cheek, I felt a little closure. That was it. It was official: the baby had passed. That day, not one person picked up the phone to call (or even text) to see how it went or how I was doing. Then two very long and lonely days went by.

The following Wednesday, we had some car trouble that resulted in Vinny having to take a day off work. We could spend some time together for the first time in quite a while—a true blessing. So we went out to breakfast.

Sitting at breakfast, I got off on a tangent about Monday, about how not one person had called me to ask how things went at the doctor's office. I told Vinny that Monday made me realize I really was going through this alone. Tears welled up in his eyes. He didn't say a word, but seeing his emotion for the first time after this miscarriage meant more to me than any words could portray. He wasn't trying to fix me; he was there with me. He understood. I was a lucky woman.

Now here's my advice to you: Tell your partner what you need *today*. If it's a shoulder to cry on, a listening ear, a night out, some fresh flowers, a bottle of wine, whatever—speak up! Don't sit back feeling sorry for yourself, like I did for so many years, miscarriage after miscarriage. I want you to learn from my mistakes. I believe that admitting my mistakes and challenges is a source of strength. I want to point them out because you can learn from them and ultimately avoid them. Don't sit around waiting, wishing, hoping for the phone to ring, for someone to stop by or for your partner to ask how you're doing today. Speak up! As I previously mentioned, miscarriages are misunderstood, so only you know what you need. Tell your partner what you really need most today.

Siblings

Brothers, sisters, stepbrothers, stepsisters, best friends you consider family—whatever your relationship—remember, unless people have personally experienced a miscarriage, it's uncommon ground, and their reactions may not be what you expect. Don't hold a grudge, because they don't know what they have or haven't done. Consider this story of my coworker (we'll call her Sarah) as an example.

Sarah is a twin. At the time, her twin sister had a one-year-old child. After her miscarriage, Sarah was ignored at work with a case of that awkward silence, so she sought comfort in family. Sarah had to have a D&C after her loss. The day after that surgery, without thinking, her twin sister gave her a calendar full of pictures of her and her firstborn child. Sarah wanted to rip that calendar up right there in front of her. *How could she be so insensitive? A baby calendar. Really? What was she thinking?* She wasn't. At the end of the day, humans can be very self-involved. Just because we didn't get much time with our baby and didn't have the opportunity to hold our precious child doesn't mean we didn't love and feel completely responsible for the little miracle growing inside us.

When family members don't recognize their harmful actions, it can be hard to forgive them. I often felt like I should point out when someone said or did something that was hurtful, but I didn't. I would think it but never speak it. What was the point? Everyone was busy, living their own lives. My loss wasn't real to them; it rarely is to outsiders. The baby was never born, it didn't have a name (well, not officially, but most definitely thought about), and it never smiled or cried. But to us, he or she was once a growing child who had stolen our hearts and changed us forever.

Again, my advice is to speak up. If you have a sibling who has been your rock and with you every step of the way, catering to your every need, thank him or her. Tell your sibling how grateful you are for the love and support. If, however, you are like Sarah, who didn't get support, even from her twin sister, speak up. I never thought to educate my family or anyone else about how I was feeling or the types of thoughts running through my mind. Maybe if I had spoke up, my brother wouldn't have delayed telling me that he and his wife were expecting until it came to the point of being obvious. Even when they did break the news, I could tell how awkward they felt, probably in fear of how I may react.

I didn't expect my family to understand, because no one else in my immediate family had experienced a miscarriage. I felt like everyone was so busy living their own lives with their own challenges that they wouldn't want to hear about mine. Looking back, I realize it wouldn't have hurt. Even if they didn't give me what I needed at the time, at least it would have been a good vent. Maybe they did care and wanted to help but didn't know what to do or say, so they were waiting until I made the first move and opened up. I didn't.

I learned from that mistake. Don't keep it all in. When you don't open up to those who love you, you fight alone. Fighting alone postpones your happiness indefinitely. Fighting alone can result in years of grieving versus finding peace with yourself a lot sooner.

Let me clarify something here: Finding peace does not mean forgetting. You will never forget. By "finding peace" I mean accepting what has happened and allowing yourself to move forward in a positive way.

Speak up today! Tell those you love how it feels to lose a child through miscarriage. What emotions are you going through? Educate them so they can understand and in turn help you.

Friends

Friends rock! Even though a close friend may not have been through a miscarriage, she is likely to know just what you need. For me, that was often a bottle of wine and a block of cheese. A good friend will let you cry and won't try to fix you. A good friend will ask how you're doing, without fear of what you might say. Friends bring flowers and give you much-needed hugs. They are probably the first people you told when you found out you were pregnant, so they heard and shared your joy as the first few weeks went by. They witnessed your joy, so they can now understand your loss.

After my first few miscarriages, I didn't take time to seek the comfort of friends. I was back at work the very next morning. But I was no good at work. I was a high school teacher, so I was not exactly the positive role model students seek in their teachers. I got upset at students for things that had never bothered me in the past. This confused them. "Are you having a bad day, Mrs. P?" a student asked one day. "Yes, I am. Do your work!" I yelled in pure anger. Poor kids. Cool Mrs. P had apparently changed her teaching methods overnight, and they didn't know what to do.

It's very important to put work aside and seek the comfort of friends. Take a few days off work. Sleep in.

Get a pedicure. Go out to lunch. Don't underestimate the healing power of retail therapy. Go out. Try to relax. You need it and you deserve it.

Many times throughout this book, you'll hear me say, "Learn from my mistakes," because I now realize I made many mistakes over the years. If I hadn't made those mistakes, which resulted in years of heartache, I probably wouldn't be writing this book for you. I probably would have assumed that, due to how common miscarriages are, every woman had a natural ability to cope with grief and continue conquering the world without a hiccup. But I came to know that we aren't all born with a grief-conquering gene, so I'm here to help you take control of your grieving. I don't want you getting stuck in a depressive state like I did.

My advice is to pick up the phone and call a trusted friend. Go on, put down the book, pick up the phone, and call a friend. Organize a dinner out for this week, invite her over, or just talk. Go on, make the call. You don't have to go through this alone.

Acquaintances

Probably the worst reaction I ever got was silence. Unfortunately, this tends to be a common reaction from acquaintances. It's that awkward moment when you return to work and you know that everyone at work *knows*, yet no one says anything. I call them "the pretenders." You walk into the office and everyone acts like it's a typical day. No sympathy cards or flowers or a simple "I'm sorry." Just silence. And people don't include you in the conversation like they did last week. It's like overnight you turned into an alien, and no one knows how to communicate with you. It's like you have an aura surrounding you that scares people away.

It's not fair. You haven't changed. You're the same person you were yesterday, but today you're grieving the loss of a child. *Just say something*, you're thinking. I might cry the second someone brings it up, but I want people to say something. Weeks may pass before work colleagues feel safe enough to reach out and express their sympathy.

It's not your fault; you aren't an alien! It's best to assume they care enough about you that they don't want to say the wrong thing and upset you, so they say nothing at all. As long as they aren't inviting you to a baby shower the day you come back (don't laugh, that actually happened), don't hold a grudge for what seem to be insensitive actions. Your colleagues most likely don't understand what you're going through and therefore figure you will bring it up if you want to talk about it.

It's your choice. Whether you want to bring it up in the workplace or not is up to you. Depending on their profession and relationships with colleagues, this choice will vary from woman to woman. If you choose not to open up the discussion at work, don't expect others to.

Time to Think

What do you really need from others? How would you like people to treat you right now? Write your true needs below. Don't hold back!

My needs:

I need a friend to call and ask how I'm doing, to tell me she's coming over to take me out.

It's your turn. What do you need?

_____

_____

_____

_____

_____

_____

Tell one person today one of these needs.

Chapter 3

Getting Back to *You*

Losing a child is a traumatic event. It's essential to take time to allow yourself to grieve. Below are some suggestions to help you through the initial stages of grief in the hope of finding some peace in this trying time. You can keep or toss any of these suggestions; some may speak to you while others don't. It's my hope that at least one or two of these suggestions help you on your journey to getting back to you.

Take Time Off

Whether you are a CEO, teacher, or personal trainer, it doesn't change the fact you're grieving the loss of a child. But work environments differ. I was a high school teacher when we went through our six miscarriages. I found out I had lost my first baby on a Tuesday afternoon, and at 7:05 a.m. Wednesday morning, I was back in the classroom in front of thirty teenagers. This was *not* a healthy situation for me or for my students. Not until I lost baby number four did I realize I needed to take some time off work. I took the rest of the week off after that miscarriage, and it made a world of difference. I didn't have to put on an act. I didn't have to try hiding the pain I was feeling. I didn't have to answer anyone's questions when they noticed I wasn't myself.

If you're in a position where you can take time away from the stress of work, please do. Take a few days to let what has happened sink in. Allow yourself to cry. You don't have to hold in the hurt and pain you're feeling. You're most likely devastated, shocked, confused, and angry. Allow the feelings, because by allowing yourself to grieve, you're giving yourself the chance to move forward.

Also slow things down. Don't set any appointments or make any commitments to be anywhere at any time for a few days.

Sometimes I thought I needed to go to work to get my mind off it. However, my mind never escaped the devastation I was feeling. It just followed me to work.

Wine a Little

Okay, so this is probably not the healthiest advice in the world, but I'm no doctor. Good friends and a bottle of wine (or two) are sometimes all we need to get ourselves back on the road to recovery. I highly recommend you give your favorite peeps a call, pick up a bottle of your favorite wine (or whatever takes your fancy), and enjoy the company. For obvious reasons, I don't recommend sitting down and drinking a bottle alone, feeling nothing but sorry for yourself, but a little social gathering can help.

I know it isn't easy to pick up the phone, and at times you just want to be alone. It definitely takes time to gather your thoughts and wrap your head around everything that's going on. When you're ready, or when you start to feel like it would be nice to talk it out, good friends and good wine are just a phone call away.

Exercise

I know you've heard it before: exercise is a great stress reliever. Well, it is! You may already be working out regularly and therefore are already gaining the physical and mental benefits of exercise. If you aren't working out regularly, now is a perfect time to start.

I was very active as a teen and young adult. I played softball back home in Australia and was given the opportunity to play professionally in Italy when I was twenty-one. I had an amazing experience and was super fit. (Man, I miss that body.) When Vinny and I settled here in the United States, it wasn't long before we decided we were ready to start a family. But after losing two babies, I was so confused about what was causing it that I started blaming everything I did. One of those things was exercise. *Maybe I shouldn't have been lifting at the gym? Maybe I shouldn't have been jogging?*

I stopped working out altogether, and my health went downhill from there. Obviously, this resulted in weight gain, combined with depression from consecutive miscarriages. My self-esteem took a tumble, and five years later, I hit rock bottom when I lost baby number six.

That was it for me. I decided it was time to make a change. I thought of the old saying "The definition of *insanity* is doing the same thing again and expecting a different result." I decided I needed to get my life back physically and mentally. My husband and I also agreed that it was time to stop trying and just let it be.

I knew it was time to go back to the gym. I needed an outlet. I needed to release my anger. I googled a CrossFit gym close to my house and gave them a call to inquire about class times and so on. The young man on the other end of the phone said, "We have classes at five, six, seven, eight, nine, ten … when are you coming in?"

"Uh," I responded. "I guess I can come in at seven tomorrow morning."

"See you tomorrow at seven. Ask for Eric."

That was it. I arrived there at seven the very next morning and have been a member for over two years now. I've met some amazing women who are now some of my closest friends. We text each other daily and hold one another accountable. Miss two days of CrossFit in a row, and I hear about it from my girls. The guilt!

For our one-year CrossFit anniversary (I swear I'm really not one of "those CrossFit people"), we competed as a team at a Tampa, Florida, fitness challenge and didn't come in last. Woo-hoo! Two months later, I had my competitive itch back and participated in my first individual CrossFit competition, finishing third in my division (beginner). You don't have to go out and join your local gym, but find something that gets you moving and makes you happy. A workout buddy makes all the difference. Gather your girls, and get moving!

Set New Goals

For five years, it was my goal to have a healthy child. I couldn't think of anything else I wanted more than to be a mother. I constantly daydreamed about who my child could be and what sports he or she would play. During the fall, I imagined what I would dress my baby up as for Halloween, and during winter I'd picture him or her opening gifts on Christmas morning. When I suffered miscarriage after miscarriage, my goal seemed to be more of a miracle than a goal I could achieve if I worked hard enough. I started to think I had more chances of winning the lotto than of having a child.

Goal setting isn't new to me. I've been writing goals since I was a teenager, and I've achieved almost every one of them. (I didn't meet my goal of marrying Matthew McConaughey, but I did marry a super-hot, amazing man, so I got over that one.) When my goal to have a child was shattered time after time, I began to lose hope. Not until I lost my sixth child did I decide it was time to start pursuing other goals. This doesn't mean I've given up on my goal to be a mother; it means for now I'm prioritizing other goals above this one. I hope you have better luck than I do. But if you're like me, maybe setting some new short-term goals is just what you need.

At the time I decided to redirect my goals and get physically and mentally healthy, I had put on a lot of weight seeking comfort in food and wine. I was heavy and depressed. There were two things I had to do to achieve these new goals: join a gym and go back on the pill.

I needed to go back on the pill to confirm that we were no longer "trying." Every month for five years, I had been playing mental games with myself, questioning every little sign that I may or may not be pregnant. If I felt tired at all, I'd get excited and question if maybe it was a sign. It was exhausting month after month, year after year. Going back on the pill helped to stop the mental games of holding on to that glimmer of hope that maybe, just maybe, I would be pregnant and this would be the one.

Two years later, I'm sitting here writing this chapter, and I feel like a new person. My mind isn't clouded. I can honestly say I'm happy. I have a zest for life again. I'm grateful every day. I smile every day. This came about only because I redirected my goals and focused on them.

We need time to recover. Working toward a different yet desired goal can help.

What have you always wanted to do but never felt you had time for? Do you want to learn how to decorate cakes, speak another language, get a degree, advance in your career, or get organized? Whatever it is, now may be the perfect time to do it.

For a while I felt guilty about "giving up." I felt like I had just quit on myself, on my goals, and on my husband. I had failed. I would justify my actions and focus on all the things I could do because I wasn't with child. I was free, I had time, and I had more money in my pocket. No more monthly copays at the OBGYN. No more expensive fertility procedures.

I realize now I didn't have to justify my decision, and you have every right to make that decision for yourself. You don't have to justify your goals. If you want something in life, set a goal and go for it. Make it happen!

List three things you've always wanted to do, learn, or accomplish.

_____

_____

_____

Write a specific and measurable goal for each of the above. It's important to be *very* specific about what you want to achieve. For example, "I want to lose ten pounds by Christmas Day," not "I want to lose weight."

Goal 1

_____

Steps I will take to achieve this goal. (Don't forget to include when you will take these steps.)

— _____

— _____

— _____

Goal 2

_____

Steps I will take to achieve this goal.

— _____

— _____

— _____

Goal 3

_____

Steps I will take to achieve this goal.

– _____

– _____

– _____

Get Your Zen On

The benefits of yoga and meditation are no secret. In recent years, a large number of yoga studios have opened in the United States, and countless books and audio CDs have been released to provide guided meditation for a large variety of reasons. Whether you need to still your mind, let go, relax, find renewed energy, or release anger, there's a guided mediation CD on the market for you today.

I know it's often difficult to find twenty minutes of uninterrupted quiet time to meditate, especially if you have small children in the house. Maybe getting out of the house for a yoga class is more realistic. Either way, I encourage you to make the time to participate in one or both of these practices. Mediation is known to

- reduce stress,
- increase happiness,
- increase acceptance,
- improve physical health, and
- improve mental health.

It's important to take time out right now—for you to love yourself without blame, to honor your body and find peace, and to allow negative emotions to escape your body.

Just recently I returned to PURE Yoga and Fitness. During my first class, I realized I'd forgotten how accepting yoga is. We are constantly reminded during the practice that it is *our* practice; we are encouraged not to look over at our neighbors but rather to practice without ego. This was quite different from CrossFit, where coaches and fellow classmates are pushing you. Don't get me wrong; both are fantastic ways to relieve stress. Choose the workout that's right for you on any given day.

During my first practice back at PURE, as we lay in a supported bridge, I felt raw emotions of sadness begin to surface. It had been two years since my last miscarriage, and I'd thought I was healed. As the instructor spoke of self-love and to be without ego, tears surfaced unexpectedly. I had forgotten how yoga not only provides the physical benefits of flexibility, circulation, and strength but also focuses on self-love and inner peace. I thank the girls at PURE for their open hearts and touching practices.

Remember, you are beautiful. You are worthy. You are strong. You are loved.

Join an Online Support Group or Blog

There are hundreds of websites offering articles, information, and support groups for women suffering the loss of a baby through miscarriage. As I searched through the sites, I found it difficult to find what I needed most: advice. That's why I wrote this book, your one-stop book of advice to help you through your time of need.

Online blogs and support groups are a great additional resource. One of my close friends really benefited from joining an online support group, where she was able to tell her story and get feedback from other women suffering the same thing. Social media is another avenue of support. You can follow me on twitter @miscarriagemom.

If you're interested in honoring your child online, check out www.aplacetoremember.com. This website allows you to write a remembrance similar to an obituary. You can create your own post to honor your baby. Here is my remembrance, which can be found on the site under B under "Remembrances."

IN MEMORY OF

PARISI BABIES

miscarried May, October, June, March, February.

Remembered by Mummy and Daddy:
Although we never got to meet you, we loved
you more than words can say. We had given
you names and planned for your arrival.
We think of you every day and know you
are all together watching over us.

Keep a Journal

Keeping a journal or diary is easy and inexpensive. There are no rules to follow. You can make it what you want. Many cute and fancy journals are on the market today, or if you're the technology type, use your computer or iPad to journal. Write a letter to yourself, to God, to your child. Or simply write about your thoughts and feelings. Use your journal to vent about anything that's bothering you. Journals are known to reduce stress as well as to clarify thoughts and emotions and help us better understand them.

Anger is a prominent emotion after a miscarriage. Writing in a journal can help release that anger, which can help you avoid taking it out on loved ones and others. Once you get going, you may find yourself going places and writing about things that you thought were unrelated. Just go with it. Rereading your entries can be a good way to reflect and to put things into perspective. When you read your words, it may help you to make sense of different events.

Journaling can be an emotional experience. I remember writing about the day I had lost my child due to an ectopic pregnancy. I cried as I typed. After that entry, I felt better. It was like I had gotten it off my chest and released it to the world. Give it a go.

Speak Up! Tell People What You Need

I've said it many times already: speak up and tell people what you really need. Tell a friend or family member how they can help you. What do you need? That's it. That's all I have to say about that one.

Make a Commitment

This chapter suggested eight ways to help get you back on track. I'm sure you had a few ideas pop into your mind as you read. Now it's time to make a commitment. What is one thing you will commit to? Remember, this is for you! For example, will you start a journal? Will you join a gym?

Today I commit to _____

_____

_____

_____

_____

I will make this happen by doing the following: _____

_____

_____

_____

_____

Chapter 4

A Man-to-Man Talk for Husbands

by Vince Parisi

The day I got the news that Kristy was pregnant, my heart leaped. A rush of adrenaline washed over me that could only be associated with the day I became an Olympian or the day I met the woman of my dreams. It was one of those days like no other. My mind started racing, thinking about all the great possibilities that lay ahead.

It was a little overwhelming to think we were about to start a new life as a family. I tried to imagine what it would feel like to be a father and put myself in my father's shoes. The time had come; I was going to have a family of my own.

Or so I thought.

Before the first miscarriage, that word never crossed my mind. My mind was where all married couples' minds are when they're expecting their firstborn. I was overwhelmed by thoughts of endless possibilities. Like many expecting parents, I thought of baby names; I wondered whether it would be a boy or a girl; I anticipated spreading the great news to friends and family members. I was excited and happy for this next phase of our lives.

I come from a very close Italian family, so we immediately told close friends and family members, who shared our joy and excitement.

Both my wife and I live a very active lifestyle. As former professional athletes, exercise has always been a huge part of our lives. When Kristy first fell pregnant, she wanted to make sure she continued an exercise routine throughout her pregnancy. Her doctor agreed that it was perfectly healthy and normal for women to continue a mild to moderate exercise program. Then came our first trip to the gym. I was working out when she came up to me sobbing and said, "We have to go." I immediately knew something terrible had happened.

In the bathroom she discovered she was bleeding. After an emergency trip to the OGBYN, we realized our worst nightmare had come true: Kristy and I had miscarried.

This was a heart-wrenching time for us. When we broke the news to close friends and family, we were surprised by their reactions. Some expressed sympathy, while others seemed not to react at all. I believe that those who didn't reach out did so because they didn't know what to say, not because they didn't care. They played it safe and said nothing at all. I believe most people are uncomfortable talking about miscarriage.

As a husband, there's nothing worse than seeing the one you love go through this. There was very little I could do to alleviate the pain and sorrow she was enduring. Yes, I was distraught, but having to see my wife distraught was the toughest part. Our close friends and family members were torn. Should they console Kristy? Should they give us space? Should they even bring it up? Since it's foreign ground for many people, they often think it's best to leave whatever unsaid.

I wish I could say that a couple of months later, Kristy fell pregnant again, and a year later we were blessed with a healthy child. A couple of months later Kristy *did* fall pregnant again and again and again. In fact, she has been pregnant and miscarried six times to date. I wish I could say it got easier with each miscarriage, but it didn't. Each got harder for Kristy to accept, making it harder and harder to cope.

As athletes, Kristy and I grew up with the notion that we could accomplish anything if we persevered and tried hard enough. So going into our second, third, fourth, fifth, and sixth pregnancies, we were under the notion that we had persevered enough and the time had finally come for us to expand our family. We are both middle children. It only made sense to us that we would have a family of our own like the ones we'd grown up in.

There's nothing worse than seeing your spouse go through the agony of miscarriage, being stripped of the opportunity to experience pregnancy and motherhood. You never think that something like that could happen— that you would be the one-in-four statistic. So, as a man and husband/partner, what do you do? Most importantly, be her shoulder to cry on. Listen without offering advice, unless asked. Let her vent, cry, and sob. Take on extra duties around the house, if possible.

After fighting off depression and the feelings of helplessness, we tried to focus on all the things we could do because we were without children. A mini vacation or weekend getaway can help. Give yourselves something to look forward to. Even if that means staying at a hotel downtown, the change in scenery can help. Also exercise is a great stress reliever. Make sure you're eating properly and not turning to fatty comfort foods and/or alcohol (which is easier said than done) to feed the pain. Focus on task-oriented daily goals that are under your control. Goal setting proved to be the best and fastest way we were able to take back control of our lives. Empathize with her. It is very important to show her you too are sad, that you are in this together.

Our marriage is stronger because of our loss. We're able to communicate on a deeper level. I can only imagine all the joys that having a child must bring, but right now, I focus on the healing process. Allow time to heal your broken heart. Time heals all things, and as we move on in life, so do our miscarried spirits. Those spirits occasionally return in many different forms as reminders of a love that was lost but will never be forgotten.

Chapter 5

How the Five Stages of Grief Apply to Your Miscarriage

Stage One: Denial

The moment you're told or know you have lost your child, you want it to be a mistake. You want the doctor to be wrong. You may demand another pregnancy test or ultrasound. Your heart seems to stop; your entire body is overwhelmed with emotion. You might think, *It can't be true. I did everything I was supposed to.*

During my very first pregnancy, I started bleeding within a week of the positive pregnancy test. Deep down, I knew what this meant, but I didn't want to believe it. On the drive to the OBGYN, I convinced myself I was one of those women who get periods during their pregnancies. Soon after arriving, it was confirmed that I had lost the baby. *Why? How? What did I do?*

You can try to deny the fact, but reality hits very quickly. And this first stage of grief is short-lived.

Stage Two: Anger

Why me? How did this happen? What did I do wrong? I didn't drink a drop of alcohol or eat anything from the deli department. Why is my baby gone?

There is rarely an answer to these questions. Many miscarriages have no medically apparent reason. It's hard not to feel like life has cheated you and to feel that you don't deserve it. Due to these thoughts, you will likely find yourself very upset and angry. I wasn't angry with myself but was angry at life. I was angry at the happy mothers at the mall. I was angry every time I saw a pregnant woman flaunting her big belly. In my mind, the anger was justified and normal.

Your anger may last a long time or come and go in certain moments. Even now I catch feelings of anger rising to the surface at unexpected times. Not so long ago, a new mother was complaining about sleepless nights with her newborn baby. I lashed out by saying, "Well, I'd rather have a healthy baby and only four hours of sleep than a restful night and no child to love."

Awkward silence.

Oops.

I have no idea where that outburst came from. It just came over me. If you're finding yourself in these moments, recognize them for what they are. If you do happen to lash out like I did, apologize immediately and let people know you're sorry and are still hurting inside from your loss. Let them know talk of babies is still very difficult for you. No one can be mad at you for apologizing and sharing a valid, heartfelt reason for your actions.

It's important to let anger out. Don't hold onto it. At times, I found myself just wanting to scream. So I did. I screamed at the top of my lungs in pure anger. Here are some suggestions to help you relieve the anger:

- Scream into a pillow.
- Write in a journal, and let all your emotions out on paper.
- Talk with a trusted friend or family member.
- Do an intense workout.
- Meditate.
- Find a place to relax.
- Call a friend and organize a night out, giving yourself something to look forward to.
- Play or listen to music.

I was angry for a very long time. Being conscious of your anger and recognizing it as a stage of grief can help you move forward.

Stage Three: Bargaining

Too often I would find myself sobbing with anger. *Why me? What did I do wrong? What more can I do?* As these questions arose, I found myself bargaining with God, the universe, a higher power. I made promises for the future if only I could be blessed with a child. It's very natural to do this.

Thinking about what you could have/should have done to prevent the miscarriage is also common. If you followed every rule for pregnancy written in every book, you would drive yourself crazy: don't eat this; eat that; exercise, but don't let your body temperature get too high; no at-home foot massages; don't stress. I remember thinking back over every meal I ate and every workout I ever did or didn't do for the duration of my pregnancy, trying to pinpoint what could have caused my miscarriage. Unfortunately, even with all the medical developments today, most miscarriages go unexplained. Don't beat yourself up about something you ate or did while pregnant. It's not your fault. It was nothing you did that caused your baby to pass. There are many beautiful quotes that can help you accept this fact. Simply google "miscarriage quotes."

An Angel in the book of life wrote
down my baby's birth.
Then whispered as she closed the book
"too beautiful for earth."
—Author unknown

At this time, you may also be thinking about all the things that could have been and how wonderful life would have been if you hadn't miscarried. I spent hours daydreaming about holding my baby, watching her open gifts on Christmas morning, teaching her how to bake cookies, and many other joyful moments I could only imagine parents get to share with their children. I say "her" because we were able to find out the sex of two of our babies after the D&Cs, and both were girls.

Imagining what could have been is nothing but heartbreaking. You can't change what has happened. Don't punish yourself with hurtful thoughts of what could have been.

Stage Four: Depression

Depression is a natural state of mind after the loss of a child. Reality settles in, and all signs of life disappear. You're no longer tired or craving eight-hundred-calorie chocolate milkshakes from Steak 'n Shake (the only craving I experienced). You feel at a complete loss. All your hopes and dreams for your baby are gone, never to see the light of day. Everyone around you seems to have fallen back into their daily routines.

What now? Depression can be the longest stage of the grieving process, especially after a miscarriage. With the loss of that physical connection, you may find yourself feeling alone.

There is an expected period of time after a miscarriage that you might feel depressed. If, however, the feelings of depression persist beyond several weeks and begin to interfere with your ability to function at home or at work, you may need to consider professional help. Signs of depression may include

- feelings of guilt, worthlessness, and/or helplessness;
- difficulty concentrating;
- insomnia or excessive sleeping;
- loss of interest in hobbies; and
- persistent sad, anxious, or "empty" feelings.

I got stuck in a depressive state for far too long—in fact, four years too long. I couldn't shake the anger and jealously I felt toward other mothers. I held on to that anger, justifying my feelings each time. Life wasn't fair. I thought, *Why am I being punished? Why can I not have a child?*

I never took the time to get professional help. Vinny and I continued to try for a baby, only to be dealt the same card over and over again. With and without medical intervention, I continued to miscarry. I was angry. I was jealous. I was depressed.

Not until I finally decided I was going to take a break from trying to get pregnant and carry a baby to term did I begin to heal. It took going back on the pill to solidify my decision. Now that there was no chance of pregnancy, I could begin to accept my reality.

Maybe you aren't ready to stop trying, and that's great! Recognize how you're feeling. Are you at peace with your recent loss? Are you filled with anger? Are you depressed? Depression is not only understandable, it is also treatable. Give yourself time and permission to grieve.

Stage Five: Acceptance

Days, weeks, maybe even months may pass before you accept the loss of your child. Once you have come to terms with your loss, you'll be able to speak of your child with greater ease. Life will begin to feel normal again. Maybe you'll start to consider trying for another child. Maybe you won't. When life feels normal again, you've reached the final stage of the grieving process. You have accepted your loss. This doesn't mean you have forgotten your child; rather, you'll feel at peace with the loss.

The time it takes to find peace varies from person to person. For me, it took over two years of taking a break to accept who I am and what I'd lost. I am a wife and mother of six angel babies. Accepting your loss will allow you to pursue other goals in life. At this point you will find renewed energy. You will get back to business. However, you will never forget; we will talk about ways to honor your baby in chapter seven.

Chapter 6

Due Dates and Holidays

As the days, months, and years pass, there will always be moments that remind you of your loss. You may suddenly find yourself overwhelmed with a feeling of emptiness or sadness.

Maybe you know the estimated due date of your baby; maybe you don't. I can remember the specific due date only of my second pregnancy: May 13. After that, I tried not to get caught up in the excitement of due dates and focused on making it through one day at a time. But naturally, as any expecting mother does, I peeked at a due date calendar at least once during each pregnancy. However, on May 13 of every year I'm saddened with thoughts of what could have been.

I think of how old she would be on that day and wonder what kinds of things she would be interested in. Would she and Addison (my niece born May 5 of the same year) be best friends? I wish I had an answer to help avoid the grief that comes on that day once a year. Sure, with time, the pain has subsided, but her spirit will live on in me forever.

My niece is a constant reminder of what I've lost. I love her dearly and treasure the time I get to spend with her. She is a true character. She loves everything princess. I wonder if my little girl would dress up as a princess every year for Halloween. Or would she be more like me at that age and prefer to play outside with the boys? It's normal to ponder these thoughts, and it's okay to cry. It can be hard to accept that our babies aren't here with us today.

The holidays can be especially hard. They can magnify our loss. When I think of Christmas, I think of children putting up the tree, visiting Santa, and opening gifts Christmas morning. I remember doing all those things when I was a child. Children keep the spirit of Christmas alive, so it's only natural to think of children during the holiday period. I've cried many times pondering Christmas with my children. Every year, it's just my husband and I putting up the tree—unless a bottle of champagne counts as company. Every year my mind wonders off with thoughts of my lost babies. How the moment feels incomplete without them there to share it with. I've considered inviting my niece over to help with the tree, but I know it won't fill the void. That and my Christmas POPD (Perfect Ornament Placement Disorder).

The holidays may be a time of year when you need to decline certain invitations if the event is centered on children—especially if your miscarriage has been recent. Try not to suppress your feelings in the name of being strong. Speak up! Talk it out. Allow yourself to release emotions that arise, so you too can have a happy holiday. You deserve it.

You can and will get through the holidays.

Chapter 7

Five Ways to Honor Your Baby

Tattoos

When I was a teen and started noticing tattoos, I said with 100 percent conviction that I would never get one. When I met my husband, he had two tattoos, and it never bothered me. After our first year of marriage, he got another three tattoos. Two of them represented our marriage, and the third is the Olympic rings tattooed on the inside of his upper right arm. (He represented Team Italy in the 2004 Athens Olympics as a member of the baseball team.) I loved his tattoos and thought that if there was something that truly meant the world to me, such as becoming an Olympian, I might get one. (My husband does mean the world to me; however, you know what I'm talking about.)

One day, while searching the Internet, I came across images for miscarriage tattoos. (If you're interested, simply google "miscarriage tattoos," select "Images," and scroll through the many pages.) There were many common images, such as baby feet, angel wings, babies with wings, and dates in roman numerals. Then I came across an image that was especially beautiful. It was a dandelion blowing in the wind, with the wisps blowing off and a few birds flying among the wisps. That was the one—the one that would honor my babies.

Keeping in mind my professional career as an educator and college professor, I wanted to put the tattoo where it wouldn't be visible in any way in the work environment. I had it placed on my middle right side, with the wisps blowing up toward my shoulder blade. Among the wisps are six birds flying off in the wind, each representing a baby.

At first I was horrified at what I had done. It was forever. However, it didn't take long before I absolutely loved my tattoo, knowing that my babies would always be with me. If I wear a dress with a low-cut back or a bathing suit, my tattoo is visible to all. If someone asks what it represents, I tell him or her. Why not? This is me, and this is my reality. I'm at a point now that I can talk about it without choking up with tears. This comes only with time.

I didn't realize how many people, especially strangers, comment and make conversation because of a tattoo. If you're placing your tattoo somewhere visible, such as on your wrist, be prepared to talk about it. Are you ready to talk about your miscarriage with a stranger? If not, consider giving yourself more time or placing the tattoo somewhere discrete.

Angels

A very common term used to describe babies lost through miscarriage is angel baby. I've always wanted to believe in angels, to hope that these beautiful souls with white wings are among us, protecting us throughout the day. After losing six babies, my desire for this to be true has grown stronger. I want to believe that my babies are angels looking over us. I'm comforted by the thought that they're still here with us in some form. This desire led me to Doreen Virtue's book *Angel Therapy.* Turns out, we *are* surrounded by angels. We can call on our angels for help, guidance, and comfort at any time.

Over a year ago, my mother-in-law gave me the book *God Is for Real* and said there was a part in the book about a miscarriage she thought I'd be interested in. Life got busy, and I never picked up the book.

One evening, I was home alone, surfing the TV for something to watch (a very rare occasion in my house), and I came across the movie *God Is for Real*. I decided to rent it, as the book was now collecting dust, and it would be quicker than reading the book (kind of like in high school when you have a test the next day and realize you haven't read the book).

In the movie, a boy visits heaven, where he meets his older sister. His parents had never mentioned her, because she was miscarried before he was born. He later returned to earth and mentioned this meeting to his parents, who were baffled that he knew about her.

The following day, my husband and I were sitting outside on our balcony, having a conversation about our children and the possibility that they're here among us. I like to think of them as a flock of beautiful birds flying peacefully among us, just as I had tattooed on my side. We had a heartfelt conversation that had us both crying.

As our conversation came to a moment of silence, a flock of six birds—not five, not seven, but six birds—flew directly over us. The timing was so perfect, it was something you'd expect to see only in a movie. We immediately looked at each other in disbelief. With tears rolling down my face, the only word I could get out was *wow.*

"Wow!"

"Wow!"

"Wow!"

I think I must have said it a hundred times.

I will never forget the moment for as long as I live. I know my babies are among us, looking over us, only a thought away.

Jewelry

Jewelry is a very personal item that we choose for ourselves or someone else. You may like to find a simple piece to wear around your neck. Or build a Pandora charm bracelet, picking charms to honor your baby and other significant moments in your life. This is less risky and permanent than getting a tattoo.

There are many beautiful charms, bracelets, necklaces, and ornaments available on the Internet, designed specifically to honor angel babies. A close friend of mine once bought me a fertility bracelet, offering the hope that one day I will be blessed with a child. It meant so much to receive such a thoughtful, heartfelt gift.

But don't sit around waiting for someone else to purchase jewelry for you. If you find something that speaks to you, get it. You deserve something to hold close and remind you of your angel.

Plant a Tree or Flower

Trees bring life. Without trees, earth would be uninhabitable. Planting a tree in memory of a loved one is a time-honored tradition that's both symbolic and heartfelt. It's a beautiful way to honor your baby and add beauty and life to your home. Find a place in your yard or garden to put a tree or flower that represents your baby. There are no rules to follow. Choose something that speaks to you. I like bright flowers, such as sunflowers and tulips. You may also like to create a plaque with a simple memorial or quote to place at the base of the plant.

Gratitude

Reflect upon your present blessings of which every man has plenty; not on your past misfortunes of which all men have some.
—Charles Dickens

I know this hardly seems to be the time and place to talk about gratitude and giving thanks. You are most likely feeling pretty low right now and thinking only of what you have just lost, not what you already have.

Eva, a close friend of mine, recently miscarried her little boy at twelve weeks. She went in for the twelve-week ultrasound, and there was no heartbeat. When she texted me to say what had happened, my heart dropped. I knew what she feeling. Immediately, images of the ultrasound rooms in which I'd been when I got the same news overwhelmed me. I remembered staring at the screen, looking at the tiny image of my baby, clearly a little human that had started to take shape. But there was no movement, no heartbeat, no sound. The doctor was silent, frantically pushing all sorts of buttons, moving the ultrasound transducer over my entire abdomen, searching for a sliver of hope. The initial news is devastating and often unexpected. At this point, you need to—and I imagine you did— allow yourself to cry, to grieve.

When out at lunch with Eva just days after she lost the baby, I was impressed by her attitude. As I drove to that lunch, I was preparing myself for some serious waterworks. I purposefully didn't put mascara on that morning in preparation for what was a sure thing to come: hugs, lunch, wine, and tears. To my surprise, she seemed okay. No tears. She was obviously not her bubbly self; rather, she was in control of her emotions.

We got to talking, and Eva said, "I know I'm lucky. I have already been blessed with a healthy little girl. We have a great life." Wow! I couldn't believe how strong and positive she was just days after her miscarriage. Being grateful for her family and everything she had helped Eva look forward.

Don't get me wrong here. If you already have been blessed with a child, that does not make your miscarriage okay. It does not mean you are grieving any less than someone without a child. The loss of a child is exactly that—the loss of a child. Regardless of any circumstance. Eva turned to being grateful for her current family as a way to cope with the loss of her little boy. By all means, she was still grieving.

There is no "at least" in child loss. Ever. Often, when people don't know what to say to a grieving mother or father, they will begin their sentence with "at least." You have likely experienced this. I sure did. *"At least you have a healthy little girl." "At least you know you can get pregnant."* It is heartbreaking to hear these comments. Unfortunately, they are very common. It was comments like this that made me feel alone and like no one understood. It is no one's place to highlight what you should be grateful for or what you already have. Only when you are ready to do it for yourself will you begin to feel the healing effects of being grateful.

There's an abundance of research highlighting that by simply giving thanks and having gratitude for what we have in life can change the outcome of our future and overall health. I highly recommend reading up on the topic. In fact, the first chapter of *The Magic* by Rhonda Byrne, the author of *The Secret*, refers to counting your blessings. She suggests that, first thing

`What I'm grateful for:

1. _____

2. _____

3. _____

4. _____

5. _____

6. _____

7. _____

8. _____

9. _____

10. _____

With Deepest Sympathy

With my deepest sympathy, this book was written to help educate, guide, and support you through your miscarriage. I hope you found comfort through my words and know you aren't alone. You can reach out to me on Twitter @miscarriagemom.

About the Author

Having personally experienced six miscarriages, Kristy Parisi understands the pain and grief of losing an unborn child. She and her husband, Vincent, have been married for ten years, spending the majority of those years trying to start a family. Both Kristy and Vincent are former professional athletes who met while playing baseball/softball in Italy.

Born and raised in Perth, Western Australia, Kristy now resides in Tampa, Florida, where Vincent grew up. She holds a master's degree in educational leadership from National Louis University.

Made in the USA
Middletown, DE
01 October 2018